Conscious Ageing

By

Barbara Frances

Conscious Ageing
Barbara Frances

Published By
Mikael Publishing
bill@mikaelpublishing.com
https://mikaelpublishing.com

All Rights Reserved

Copyright 2021 Barbara Frances

ISBN: 9781951776688

Contents

Introduction   1

Conscious Ageing   3

Reflections On Turning 80   13

About Barbara   17

Introduction

Just prior to my 80th birthday, I came across this essay written somewhere in my early 50s. First off, I was impressed with my fifty-something self. She was deep and optimistic. Secondly, I experienced a deep thanksgiving that I'm not scuttling along the hallway of a nursing home clutching my daughter's arm, not fully aware of where I am or who she is.

I believe that my fifty-year-old self sowed some powerful seeds that have allowed me to grow into my eighty-year-old self. However, there have been things she couldn't foresee that have altered aspects of herself. When I turned seventy, I had a big party and danced most of the night away. That won't happen at this birthday. In my mid-seventies, I developed some health issues which have changed me. I'm doing well, but I've had to accept that this body is deteriorating. In addition, this country and the world are deteriorating and have become frightening places to live. Many people voted for an amoral person to act as our president. A gang of thugs desecrated our Congress. Climate change is irreversible for the most part. A pandemic swept over this planet and killed thousands and thousands. I lived through the 60s and 70S, witnessed and was a part of great positive changes amidst turmoil, yet we felt that in the end good would triumph. But not so this time, because evil has become the dominant force.

So, I'd like to go back in time and tell my fifty-something self that no matter how much care we take for ourselves, (which by the way I still do) outer circumstances can impede our physical vigor, cloud our mental outlooks, create emotional discord, and jade our spiritual awareness.

Conscious Ageing

Scooting along beside me, mother clutches my arm tightly as I guide her down the hall of the nursing home. I stop at a doorway. "Here's your room, Mom." She looks blankly, then nods and shuffles within, confident that I know the way. My mother has Alzheimers. I am now her mother. I straighten her drawers, pay her bills, buy her clothes, see that she's content, and hold her in my arms and comfort her. She's been in a nursing home for a little over a year: a place where, at one time, I had said I'd never put a parent of mine. But life doth make liars of us all. She's in there and I'm out here, learning.

Learning what old age can be, while carefully evaluating the present and how I want my present to create a different future for myself. I have arrived at that time in life where I can see and even accept the final curtain of my existence on this plane. It's neither foreign nor scary to me. I realize I will not eternally "strut and fret" upon this stage. This realization is one of the blessings of passing through the forties and into the fifties. Nevertheless, quiet waves of fear do wash over me when I consider what might occur before that curtain drops. Will I be dependent, helpless, depressed? Or will I be vibrant, independent, alert? Can I avoid my mother's fate and the fate of all those who, like her, are spending their "golden" years under the complete care of others. Those countless ones who've lost independence, and, God help us, dignity.

Do I have a choice as to how I age? I believe I do. Several months ago as the hot sun of a central Texas June was bidding adieu to the day, I joined a group of people who had gathered together in a cave to look at choices and decisions we can make now, concerning the last phase of our sojourn. We were mostly strangers, but we all knew each other intimately; we not only could sense each other's fears about ageing but also could feel the hopes and determinations that lay close to each out forty to over seventy-year-old hearts. Just to show up for an event of this sort, each of us had somewhat overcome and even spurned the media and society's indictments on ageing. We came together to see how we could change those charges into values and rewards.

So we assembled beneath the earth to reconnect with our Mother, our Source, and we had rituals, the soul food that has all but been eliminated in our fast-paced, high-tech, "doing" world. We journey ahead. We fed our souls with the food we'll need to nourish us on the journey ahead. We called forth our ancestors to assist us; we faced and embraced our shadow; we got in touch with that eternal part of us, the spirit that quickens our bodies with the same vigor and zest as when we were infants, never changing, always present.

I, along with my newfound friends, left the womb of the Mother that night changed, hopeful, and excited about the great roadway available to us. A roadway that we can build. The next day, we again gathered. This time in a large meeting room with stone walls and floor-length windows overlooking a park, resplendent with rolling lawns, ancient trees, and newly budded flowers. From this meeting, I was able to sort out some of my deep feelings and bring them up to the light of consciousness.

I came to know that I can make choices now that will determine the outcome of my life. Not to say that my mother and those who are with her, chose to be where they are. But. I don't think my mother ever chose not to be where she is. She, like so many, looked upon ageing, with its unfavorable consequences as inevitable. On some deep level, she accepted feebleness, senility, illness, and yes, even humiliation, as a nature part of the end of life. Like her, I grew up with the "over the hill", "can't teach an old dog", and "spring chicken" rhetoric with all its destructive implications. Yet, I know that I don't have to accept those beliefs. Just as I cast aside the orthodox religious creed my community felt I needed as a child, I now cast to the ethers the indoctrinations that our collective consciousness has ascribed to ageing.

So what do I choose in their place: I have come to know from the inside out that what I sow today, I will reap tomorrow. So what are the seeds I wish to begin sowing now, so that I can look forward to a rich, full harvest in the days to come. The other day I recalled an incident years ago when I was teaching a poetry unit in high school English. I told my students with the bravado of a thirty-three-year-old that I was going to live until I die, bypassing old age and I didn't intend to check out early. I explained that "to live", I meant to be aware, carefree, joyful, zestful. The students were already so imbued with society's beliefs that they argued. I couldn't have it both ways. Already at such an early age, they could not equate "living fully" to a person in the seventies or eighties, and certainly not the nineties. It still saddens me when I think of their responses, and still, how many times lately haven't I also bought into that consciousness: Yet to live until I die is very much as a basic part of my philosophy today. I choose to live each moment with awareness, zest, and joy. So I sow this seed of intention to live every moment fully now in the present and the next present and the next present, on and on down the corridor of every flowing years.

Secondly, I sow the seed of nurturing and caring for my body. I nourish it with good food and exercise. By exercise, I don't mean going from my desk to the refrigerator and back again. I mean getting serious about a program, putting on the jogging shoes, the leotard and tights and going to aerobics class. My exercise program tends to rotate with the seasons; yoga, weightlifting, swimming, walking, and sometimes Richard Simmons in the living. Too many people who know far more than I do about the body have convinced me that exercise is absolutely essential for long, energetic body maintenance. I also work on doing the little niceties for my body, like drinking the eight glasses of water daily, flossing the teeth every night, and putting cream on every inch of skin after my shower. The body really delights in the small amenities.

Next, I plant the seeds of stimulation for the mind. I try to make it a point to learn something new every day, whether it be a vocabulary word or a phrase in a foreign language. I read a lot and talk with people who also read a lot. Several of my friends have started college or are going back to college. What better time! One friend was studying for a math exam while baking cookies for her grandchildren, who were on their way over to her house. I cherish that image: a flour dusted math book propped up on a kitchen counter, energetic hands that alternate between beating the eggs and butter and flipping pages, a mind jumping from ginger snaps to equations, keeping both in perfect order. This picture shows me we don't have to dismiss what our grandmothers did, and yet we don't have to sacrifice ourselves for the past. We can have both.

As I cast my seeds out, I am very careful to embed strong ones for my emotional self. I avoid stress whenever possible for this particular self, striving always to arrange my life conditions in harmony, peace, and order. I've come to realize that arguing is pointless, so I let go of a need to be right and avoid argumentative people. For the stresses I can't avoid, I pray and meditate, which gets into another seedling that I will come back to.

Also, I feed myself aesthetically with good music, plays, movies, walks in nature, tours of buildings of inspired architecture, art galleries, to name a few. This food connects me with that part in myself that longs for and savors beauty. To air out and live my emotional self, I seek to recapture my sense of play. Our natural state is in play. Look at the children. So I focus on being in that natural state; playing while I clean house while I write, while I'm being serious. I remember doing that as a child, playing at being serious. It was great fun because that was the game that made me feel most grown up. With play comes laughter, carefreeness, generosity, openness, love—a balanced emotional body.

Lastly, I shall press onto that fertile ground the seeds of a growing realization. Realization of my source, my purpose, and my connection to all life, the seen as well as the unseen; the past, present and future. For this too I have a program—I meditate at least twice a day and I pray daily. It doesn't matter who I pray to, "many names, one God"; the importance is the prayer.

Through meditation and prayer, we connect with that part of ourselves that is eternal.

So what are my choices? I choose to be:
1. Physically strong and vigorous

2. Mentally expanding and exploring

3. Emotionally harmonious

4. Spiritually aware

Our group is going to come together again and yet again. Perhaps we'll have to keep going at it for years to come because, after all, we are foraging new terrain. Our numbers are small now, but our ideas, like all good ideas, will catch on and we will redefine the process of ageing.

Reflections on turning 80

Eighty years–eight decades...A crone of the clan, at last.

I whole heartedly embrace the role of crone, the wise woman, the still woman, the reflective woman. I'm very fortunate to have reached this state and do not take it lightly.

I've had to experience great joys and suffer great griefs to arrive at this state. I've had to learn how to love unconditionally and how to assuage base hatreds. I've had to learn how to forgive and how to walk away. I've learned how to accept what is inevitable and reject what does not serve me. And I have learned that I have infinitely more to learn, and I am a ready student.

In human time, I suppose eighty years is a rather long time, but in universe time, it's less than the blink of the eye. This gives me a realization of my overall unimportance in the whole scheme of ongoing existence. Which is good.

At 80, I realize there are no concrete answers to the profound questions. There are only beliefs, guesses and fantasies that come and go with the changing seasons for those, who like me, continue to wonder and question. Fortunately, at 80, I no longer need answers. I'm perfectly content to live in the unknowing, the continual questioning, the awesome wondering.

I feel I really understand what Shakespeare meant when he said, "There are more things in the heaven and earth than are dreamt of in your philosophy." Those words give me peace. The unknowing, the questioning, the wondering.

I have acquired wisdoms, however. They are:

a) The only fortunes worth having are inner peace, stillness, and contentment. And one can acquire these no matter what the outer circumstances are.

b) Simplicity is the gold which adorns our inner peace. Simplicity in things, possessions, relationships, ideas, goals and beliefs. I find it easier and easier to say, "You can go now," whether it's a person who no longer brings me happiness, or a thing which no longer serves my needs. I have learned to keep my needs simple. The less I want, the less discontent I feel.

c) Gratitude is the crowning jewel of a life filled with inner peace. Thank you, thank you, thank you. A spiritual teacher once told me that the only prayer one needs to say is, "thank you."

So now I want to thank each of you for bringing me love.

What about love? At 80, I feel I'm beginning to understand what the great teachers, Jesus, the Buddha, Krishna and so on, meant when they spoke of love. It's not a feeling that comes from within. Rather, it's a state of being which encompasses all. That's the best I can do in defining it. In short, words fail. It's a mystery.

About Barbara

Barbara Frances has plenty of stories and a life spent acquiring them. Growing up Catholic on a small Texas farm, her childhood ambition was to become a nun. At age fourteen, she entered a convent boarding school as an aspirant, the first of several steps before taking vows. The Sisters were disappointed, however, when she passed up the habit for the University of North Texas, where she graduated with a bachelor's degree in English and Theatre Arts.

Her professors were similarly disappointed when she passed up a postgraduate degree to become a (stewardess) flight attendant. Barbara, however, never looked back. "In the Sixties, a flight attendant was a glamorous occupation." Some highlights included an evening on the town with Chuck Berry and "opening the bar" for a planeload of young privates on their way to Vietnam.

Barbara eventually returned to Texas and settled down. Marriage, children, school teaching and divorce distracted her from storytelling, but one summer she and a friend coauthored a screenplay. "I never had such fun! I come from a family of storytellers. Relatives would come over and after dinner, everyone would tell tales. Sometimes they were even true."

The next summer, Barbara wrote a screenplay on her own. Others followed, including Two Women, a finalist in the 1990 Austin Screenwriters Festival. Three more were optioned: Silent Crossing, The Anniversary and Sojourner Truth.

Barbara left teaching and continued to work on her screenplays. In 1992, exhausted by endless rewrites, she did something many screenwriters threaten but few carry out. She turned down an option renewal, done forever with writing—or so she thought.

It was not to be. One day a friend's child found and read Lottie's Adventure, her script for a children's movie. At her young fan's urging, Barbara turned it into a book entitled Lottie's Adventure: Facing The Monster, published by Positive Imaging, LLC. For her next book, Like I Used to Dance, Barbara drew upon childhood memories and "front porch stories." Her next novel was a Southern Gothic tale entitled Shadow's Way, about a woman caught in the struggle to keep her beloved plantation home from a vengeful archbishop. The Sisters might be appalled but her readers love it. Now she's working on a memoir due to be published in January, 2022. Soon you can learn more about

this memoir on her website at
https://barbarafrances.com .

Barbara's fans can be thankful she passed up
convent life for one of stories and storytelling.
She and her husband Bill live in Austin, Texas.
She can be reached at
barbfrances2006@gmail.com .

Made in the USA
Middletown, DE
23 June 2023

33330670R00015